Mini-Moments
for
Mothers

Mini-Moments
for
Mothers

by Robert Strand

New Leaf Press

First printing: February 1996
Second printing: May 1996

ISBN: 0-89221-316-7
Library of Congress Catalog No. 95-73130

Presented to:

_____

Presented by:

_____

Date:

_____

Tell Me!

Quite soon after her baby brother was born, little Ellie began begging her parents to let her be alone with the new baby. They, naturally, were a bit worried that like most four and one-half year olds, she must be feeling some jealousy and might do him some harm, so they said "no." But as they observed her and baby brother they detected no signs of jealousy. When she had the opportunity, she treated the baby with kindness. As a few days went by her pleas to be left alone with him became more and more insistent. They finally decided to allow it.

Happy, she went into the baby's room and shut the door . . . but Mom and Dad followed and opened it a crack, just enough for curious parents to look in and observe. They watched as little Ellie tiptoed up to her baby brother, put her face down close to his, cheek touching cheek, and said, "Baby, tell me what God feels like. I'm starting to forget."

A mother should be like a quilt . . . keep the children warm but don't smother them.

He tends his flock like a shepherd: He gathers the lambs in His arms and carries them close to his heart; He gently leads those that have young (Isa. 40:11).

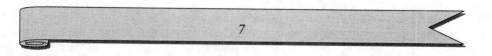

Growth

The landscape gardener looked surprised, "Will you say that again, ma'am?"

The lady of the house waved a hand to include the several-acre woodland she was having landscaped, "I want a picture of how it will all look when it's finished . . . fish pond and rose garden included. Could it look like this sketch in *Better Homes and Gardens?*"

"Hard to say, you know," the gardener said, "we're dealing with living things. I can show you a pattern, I guess, but these things grow. Okay? So you're going to have to keep on planting, cultivating, and trimming. Who's to say what it will look like someday? It's just never going to get finished growing."

Later, the lady, explained to her friend, "I had no idea I was hiring a philosopher, but that little speech reminded me that growth doesn't stop when we or our kids reach our full height."

Simply having children does not necessarily
make a woman a mother.

*Listen my son, to your father's
instruction and do not forsake your
mother's teaching. They will be a
garland to grace your head and a
chain to adorn your neck* (Prov. 1:8-9).

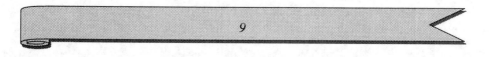

*God can't always be everywhere,
and so He invented mothers.*

Sir Edwin Arnold (1832–1904)

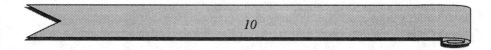

Honking Horns

It could have happened in your town. A lady driver was having difficulty getting her car started after it had stalled in traffic at a light. The gentleman (using the term loosely) in the car immediately behind her insisted on expressing his impatience with her by blowing his horn, loudly and insistently.

Finally, this lady, worn out by his thoughtfulness, stepped out of her car, walked back to the honker's car and said, "I am having a bit of difficulty in getting my car started. If you'll go and see if you can start it, I'll be glad to honk your horn for you!"

I love it! A whole lot of folks in your town, in your church, in your clubs, do much more honking than helping. There are always more talkers than workers. More critics than builders. Anyone who drives much will get honked at . . . and anyone who tries to accomplish something of value will find horn-honkers.

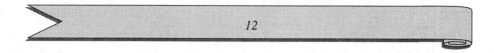

A mother's patience is like a tube of
toothpaste . . . it's never quite all gone.

*We also rejoice in our sufferings,
because we know that suffering
produces perseverance; perseverance,
character; and character, hope*
(Rom. 5:3-4).

The Real Story

Asked by his mother what he'd learned in Sunday school, ten-year-old Jimmy launched into an exciting story. "Teacher told us about when God sent Moses behind the enemy lines to rescue the Israelites from the Egyptians. When they came to the Red Sea, Moses called for the engineers to build a pontoon bridge. And after they had all crossed, they looked back and saw the Egyptian tanks coming. Moses radioed headquarters to send bombers to blow up the bridge and save the Israelites!"

"Jimmy!" said his mother. "Is that really the way your teacher told you that story?"

"Well, not exactly," Jimmy admitted, "but if I told it her way, you'd never believe it!"

In the minds of most adults, Sunday school is a place for kids. But it's more than that. It's a place for adults, as well as being a great support system for reinforcing life principles.

Children brought up in Sunday school are
seldom brought up in court.

*Train a child in the way he should go,
and when he is old he will not turn
from it* (Prov. 22:6)

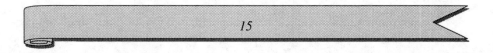

The Master Note

Have you heard the story of a shepherd in the mountains of Idaho, who was a listener to one of the finer musical programs on the radio? One night after listening to the concert, he wrote a letter to the radio station in which he made a most unusual request.

The letter said in part: "I enjoy your program from Los Angeles every week and I am writing to ask you a favor. It's rather lonely up here in the hills and I haven't much to entertain me except listening to the radio. I have an old violin which I once could play, but it has gotten badly out of tune. I wonder if you would take just a moment on your program next week to strike 'A' on the piano, so that I may tune my violin?"

At first they smiled at the letter, but honored the request when the next program of concert music came on the air. What's so important about an "A" note? Musicians tell me it's the master note on which all the rest of music is founded. And in life, Jesus Christ, is that master note!

Christianity is not a religion, it is a
relationship. (Dr. Thieme)

*"But what about you?" he asked.
"Who do you say I am?" Simon Peter
answered, "You are the Christ, the Son
of the living God"* (Matt. 16:16-17).

Let your home be your parish,
your little brood your congregation,
your living room a sanctuary,
and your knee a sacred altar.

Billy Graham (1918–)

Forgiveness

Florence Littauer has written a book, *After Every Wedding Comes a Marriage.* I'll lift one quote from it: "I used to gather up my husband Fred's faults with the fervor of a child picking berries. I had a whole shelf of overflowing baskets before the concept of forgiveness fell heavily upon me. To be spiritual I plucked out a few of Fred's faults and forgave them, but I didn't want to clear the whole shelf. Where would I go for future reference material?"

Good question! In order to make any kind of human relationship work, there must be forgiveness as part of the mix someplace. We all make mistakes. Many things in life cannot be "made right." The only answer for the human blundering and living is an honest act of forgiveness. It's outrageously costly . . . this cutting away from a person their wrong and letting them go free. But there is no other way to meaningful, honest, open, healing, wonderful relationships!

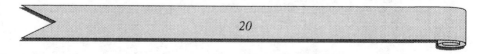

She who cannot forgive others breaks the
bridge over which she must pass herself.
(George Herbert)

*Forgive us our debts, as we also have
forgiven our debtors* (Matt. 6:12).

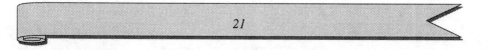

Newborns

A small boy came home from school to ask his mother that question which all parents dread: "Mommy, where did I come from?"

His mother sat down and in simple language carefully tried to tie together the birds and the bees, the stork and the local obstetric ward. The boy listened with rapt attention until she had finished her lengthy, halting monologue. Then he said, "That's nice, Mommy. But that new boy, Eric, said he came from Atlanta. Where did I come from?"

Birth is a fascinating subject. Mothers rehash their horror stories of morning sickness and labor pains . . . fathers recall with charming inaccuracy their calm cool-headed assistance to a pregnant wife in the labor room. Natural births can't be rushed, neither can spiritual births. Jesus compared the entering of the kingdom of God to the natural birth process.

If you are born once, you die twice . . . if you
are born twice, you die once.

*Jesus answered, "I tell you the truth,
no one can enter the kingdom of God
unless he is born of water and Spirit.
Flesh gives birth to flesh, but the Spirit
gives birth to the spirit. You should not
be surprised at my saying, 'You must
be born again' "* (John 3:5-7).

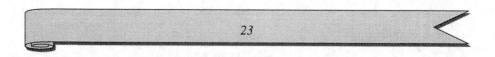

Tired

A man arrived home for the evening to find his wife, mother of his children, sprawled out on the couch, obviously bushed. She looked up at him and said: "I'm tired. Today my heart beat 103,369 times, my blood traveled 168 million miles, I breathed 23,400 times, I inhaled 438 cubic feet of air, I ate two pounds of food, I drank 1.9 pounds of liquids, I perspired .43 pints, I gave off 85.3 degrees of heat, I generated 450 tons of energy, I spoke 24,800 words, I moved 750 major muscles, my nails grew .0005 (10,000s) of an inch, my hair grew .017 (thousands) of an inch, and I exercised seven million brain cells! That's why I'm tired tonight! Do you mind if I just relax a bit?"

What a wonderful machine the human body is! Who should have the credit for such a marvel? How about giving God a bit of praise and thanksgiving? I'm for living with a grateful heart for what has been given us.

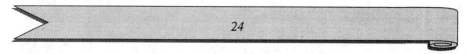

Things have changed with doctors . . . they used to check our pulse, nowadays they check our purse.

*I praise You because I am fearfully and
wonderfully made; Your works are
wonderful, I know that full well*
(Ps. 139:14).

*A mother understands
what a child does not say.*

Jewish Proverb

Yes, You Are

A mother was having a hard time getting her son out the door and on his way to school one morning. Her son complained, "Nobody likes me at school. The teachers don't and the kids don't. The superintendent wants to transfer me, the bus drivers hate me, the school board wants me to drop out, and the custodians have it in for me. I don't want to go!"

"You've got to go," insisted his mother. "You're healthy. You've got a lot to learn. You've got something to offer others. You're a leader. Besides you are 44 years old. You have to go to school because you're the principal of the thing!"

School . . . how we all need it but hate to go. We like the end results of an education but none of us really likes the process. And how about a word of appreciation for schoolteachers and administrators . . . then follow it up with a prayer for them.

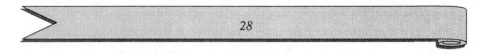

School days can be the happiest days of your life . . . if your kids are old enough to attend.

These commandments that I give you
today are to be upon your hearts.
Impress them on your children. Talk
about them when you sit at home and
when you walk along the road, when
you lie down and when you get up
(Deut. 6:6-7).

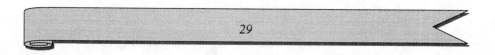

TV and the Doctor

If Dr. William Dietz had his way, another well-loved product found in American homes would carry this warning label: "WARNING . . . TELEVISION VIEWING MAY BE HAZARDOUS TO YOUR HEALTH!"

Dietz, chairman of the American Academy of Pediatrics' sub-committee on children and television, said that TV is hazardous because too many parents have no control over its use and no idea what its messages are.

The average child watches three to five hours daily . . . 15,000 hours by the time he or she is 18 compared to only 11,000 hours in the classroom! According to his research, the tube instructs kids: to be aggressive toward others (the average child has seen 18,000 televised murders while growing up); that drugs, booze, and cigarettes are a good way to deal with life problems; and that sex, while exciting, carries no responsibility.

As a result, this academy recommends severe limitations on television viewing!

A child's definition of a torture chamber is a family rec room without a TV set.

The god of this age has blinded the minds of unbelievers, so that they cannot see the light of the gospel of the glory of Christ, who is the image of God (2 Cor. 4:4).

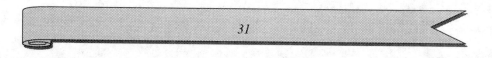

Not Worthwhile

A young lady was riding on a city bus, it was crowded, and the only empty seat was beside her. Later she described to her friend how this particular lady had plunked herself down, then crammed in a bird cage, a basket of apples, and three or four more bundles and had literally shoved her out into the aisle.

"Why didn't you tell her she was taking more than her share of the room and encroaching on your rights?" asked her friend.

This was her reply: "It wasn't worthwhile to trouble about it, we had such a little way to go together."

What a life concept to live with! Many of life's little annoyances, in reality, are not worth noticing. So many small unkindnesses simply need to be overlooked. The next time you are cut off at a stop light or pushed out of line in the grocery check-out line, remember the life philosophy of this kind young lady for living above annoyances!

Now there's even a book on the market for people who are disagreeable . . . a "Contra-dictionary."

But the wisdom that comes from heaven is first of all pure; then peace-loving, considerate, submissive, full of mercy and good fruit, impartial and sincere. Peacemakers who sow in peace raise a harvest of righteousness (James 3:17-18).

A Lie

A thoughtful little girl was talking to her mother, asking, "Which is worse, Mom, to tell a lie or to steal?"

The mother replied that both were a sin and she could not tell which was the worse, because both were bad. "Well, Mother," replied the little one, "I've been thinking about this a lot. I think it's worse to lie than to steal."

"Honey, please tell me why," her mother asked.

"Well, you see, Mother, it's like this," said the little girl. "If you steal a thing, you can take it back, unless you've eaten it and if you've eaten it, you can pay for it . . . but a lie is forever."

Smart little girl. A lie can destroy reputations, ruin relationships, and destroy trust. Both lying and stealing can be forgiven and the only eternal forgiveness is found in Jesus Christ.

Other people can usually determine your character by observing what you stand for, fall for, and lie for.

You shall not steal. You shall not give
false testimony against your neighbor
(Exod. 20:15-16).

*Motherhood is the greatest
privilege of life.*

May R. Coker

The Wrong Place

Ever been at the wrong place at the wrong time? Consider:
Patricia Spahic, age 59, who was sitting in the third row during a
Pittsburgh production of *Hamlet* in 1989. She was cut on the head
when Hamlet's dagger slipped out of his hand and sailed into the
audience!

Or . . . Joan Raeburn, age 26, of West Harrison, Indiana, who
was traveling by car on a rural road near the Ohio state line in 1987.
She was the victim of a hit-and-run pilot, who grazed the roof of her
car with his single-engine airplane and flew off into the night!

Or . . . the mother who was shot and killed while lying in her
bed in her Austin, Texas, apartment in 1988. The man downstairs had
fired a loaded pistol up through the ceiling by accident.

It's best in this life, uncertain as it is, to be sure that our life
insurance is paid up as well as our eternal life assurance plan — for
living in readiness for any uncertainty.

Let us live as people who are prepared to die,
and die as people who are prepared to live.
(James S. Stewart)

*Just as man is destined to die once,
and after that to face judgment, so
Christ was sacrificed once to take
away the sins of many people; and He
will appear a second time, not to bear
sin, but to bring salvation to those who
are waiting for Him* (Heb. 9:27-28).

Baking a Cake

Some unknown, unsung mother has written, "How to Bake a Cake." Here's what she wrote: Preheat oven; get out utensils and ingredients . . . remove blocks and toy cars from table . . . grease pan, crack nuts; measure two cups of flour; remove baby's hands from flour, wash flour off baby. Re-measure flour. Put flour, baking powder and salt in sifter. Get dustpan and brush up pieces of bowl baby knocked on the floor. Get another bowl. Answer doorbell. Return to kitchen. Remove baby's hands from bowl. Wash baby. Answer phone. Return. Remove one-fourth inch of salt from greased pan. Look for baby. Grease another pan. Answer phone. Return to kitchen and find baby. Remove hands from bowl . . . take up greased pan and find layer of nutshells in it. Head for baby, who flees, knocking bowl off table. Wash kitchen floor, table, walls, dishes, and baby. CALL LOCAL BAKERY! Lie down with baby for a nap.

And what more need be added, other than to take time to enjoy the baby when still a baby.

A baby is a puckered and trembling
lower lip, trying hard . . . oh, so hard,
to tell you something.

Sons are a heritage from the Lord,
children a reward from Him
(Ps. 127:3).

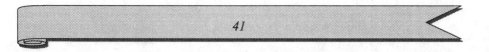

Today's Family

Those who are preparing to celebrate the downfall of the traditional family probably should put away the party hats. The good news is that it's a premature celebration. CONSIDER: 92 percent of those interviewed in a recent Gallup Poll said they had never been unfaithful to their spouses! Ninety-two percent! Further, 83 percent said they would marry the same partner again. Seventy-six percent said they pray together as a family! Gallup's conclusion: "Marriages today are stronger than previously believed."

In a separate survey of 1,000 people, *Parents* magazine reported that 78 percent expressed a desire to return to "traditional values and old-fashioned morality!"

Now, that's what I call good news for a good day! So, hang in there, Mom, and don't believe everything negative you hear from the media about the downfall of families!

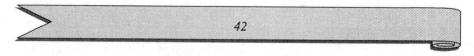

A family altar would alter many a family.

God is our refuge and strength, an
ever-present help in trouble. Therefore
we will not fear, though the earth give
way and the mountains fall into the
heart of the sea (Ps. 46:1-2).

Youth fades; love droops;
the leaves of friendship fall.
A mother's secret love outlives them all.

Oliver Wendell Holmes (1809–1894)

Don't Quit

When things go wrong as they sometimes will;
When the road you're trudging seems all uphill;
When the funds are low, and the debts are high;
And you want to smile but you have to sigh;
When care is pressing you down a bit . . .
Rest if you must, but don't quit!

SUCCESS is failure turned inside out;
The silver tint of the clouds of doubt;
And you never can tell how close you are . . .
It may be near when it seems afar.
So stick to the fight when you're hardest hit . . .
It's when things go wrong that you mustn't quit!
(Author unknown)

Consider the postage stamp — its usefulness consists of the ability to stick to one thing until it gets there. (Samuel Johnson)

Love does not delight in evil but rejoices with the truth. It always protects, always trusts, always hopes, always perseveres (1 Cor. 13:6-7).

Go Home

Judge Phillip Gilliam of Denver recently gave this advice to the young people of his city in response to their cry: "What can we do? Where can we go?"

"Go home!" says the Judge. "Hang the storm windows, paint the woodwork, rake the leaves, mow the lawn, wash the car, learn to cook, scrub the floors, repair the swing, build a boat, get a job, help the poor, study your lessons . . . and when you are through and not too tired, read a good book!"

Pretty good, homespun, plain, down-to-earth, nitty-gritty kind of advice. Not spectacular but it works! Maybe we as parents have been too lenient with this current generation. We all know that a good work ethic is one of the foundational building blocks of a productive life. I'm for helping young people develop a work ethic.

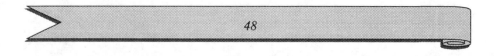

All play and no work makes Jack and Jill a
big taxpayer's bill.

We hear that some among you are idle.
They are not busy; they are busy-
bodies. Such people we command and
urge in the Lord Jesus Christ to settle
down and earn the bread they eat
(2 Thess. 3:11-12).

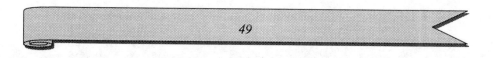

Recognition

"I don't want to hear
    another word!"
I hear my daughter scold.
"Dear me!" I think, "She's
    awfully strict
For a playful three year old.

She rolls her eyes heavenward
And sighs with great disdain
"What am I going to do
    with you?"
Her dolls hear her complain.

"Sit down! Be still! Hold out
    your hands!
Do you have to walk so slow?
Pick up your toys! Go
    brush your teeth!
Eat all your carrots! Blow!"

I start to tell her how gentle
    A mother ought to be
When blushingly, I realize
    She's imitating ME!
    (Author Unknown)

Motherhood is hereditary . . . chances
are if your parents didn't have children,
you won't either.

*"Honor your father and mother" —
which is the first commandment with a
promise — "that it may go well with
you and that you may enjoy long life
on the earth" (Eph. 6:2-3).*

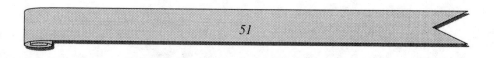

*No man is poor
who has had a godly mother.*

Abraham Lincoln (1809–1865)

What Some Famous Mothers Could Have Said

Alexander the Great's Mother: "How many times do I have to tell you . . . you can't have everything you want in this world."

Franz Schubert's Mother: "Take my advice, son. Never start anything you can't finish."

Sigmund Freud's Mother: "Stop pestering me! I've told you many hundreds of time that the stork brought you."

Boy George's Mother: "Do you enjoy being different? Just why can't you be like Nancy, your brother?"

Ben Franklin's Mother: "How many times do I have to tell you that you cannot fly your kite in a rainstorm!?"

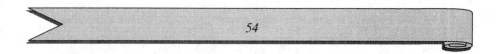

An ounce of mother is worth a pound of clergy. (Spanish Proverb)

Adam named his wife Eve, because she would become the mother of all the living (Gen. 3:20).

The Beauty of Mother

It was mid-October and the trees along the beautiful, winding Lovers Lane Boulevard in St. Joseph, Missouri, were absolutely gorgeous with color! This parkway had been planted with maple trees, now grown and reaching to each other over the road. We were walking and came to a stop next to a lady who was showing the view to her elderly mother. "Isn't it wonderful of God to take something just before it dies and is gone and make it so beautiful?" the daughter was commenting as she looked at the falling leaves.

"Wouldn't that be nice if He also did that with people?" the mother replied, deep in thought.

The younger lady, turned to look at the stooped, aged, white-haired, gentle-faced, mother beside her. She smiled and answered so softly that she must have thought no one else could have heard, "Sometimes He does."

I finally found a Mother's Day card that expressed my feelings for my mother in real terms. It said, "Now that we have a mature, adult relationship, there's something I'd like to tell you. You're still the first person I think of when I fall down and go boom!"

A wise son brings joy to his father, but
a foolish man despises his mother
(Prov. 15:20).

Not Too Far Off

It was a special "Rally Day" program at the church and a little girl was to recite the Scripture verse which she had memorized for the occasion. When she got in front of the crowd, the sight of all those eyes peering at her caused her to forget her memorized Bible verse.

Every line which she had so carefully rehearsed faded and she stood there unable to utter a single word. In the front row, her mother was almost as frantic as the little girl. The mother gestured, moved her lips, trying to form the words for the little one. No good.

Finally, the mother in desperation, whispered the opening phrase of the memorized Bible verse: "I am the light of the world."

Immediately the child's face lit up, relaxed, and a smile appeared as she said with supreme confidence: "My mother is the light of the world!"

A minister gives this perfect tribute: "My mother practices what I preach!"

Samuel was ministering before the Lord . . . a boy wearing a linen ephod. Each year his mother made him a little robe and took it to him when she went up with her husband to offer the annual sacrifice (1 Sam. 2:18-19).

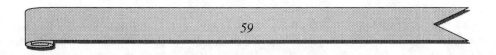

Thank You, God,
For pretending not to notice that one of
Your angels is missing and for guiding her to me.
You must have known how much I
would need her, so
You turned Your head for a minute
and allowed her to slip away to me.
Sometimes I wonder what special name
You had for her.
I Call her "Mother."

Bernice Maddux

Some Notes for Mothers

Dear Mother: I am going to make dinner for you for Mother's Day. It's going to be a surprise." Your daughter, Angie. P.S. I hope you like pizza and popcorn.

Dear Mother: I got you a turtle for Mother's Day. I hope you like the turtle I got you this year better than the snake I got you for Mother's Day last year. Your son, Robert

Dear Mother: "I wish Mother's Day wasn't always on Sunday. It would be better if it was on Monday so we wouldn't have to go to school. Love, Aileen

Dear Mother: I hope you like the flowers I got you for Mother's Day. I picked them myself when Mr. Smith wasn't looking. Your daughter, Diane

Dear Mother: Here are two aspirins. Billy and I promise not to fight all day. Have a happy Mother's Day. Your son, Arthur

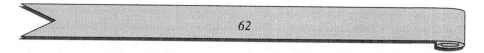

Mom, Today is Mother's Day, so don't bother with the dishes. Leave them. You can always wash them tomorrow. (From your kids)

He settles the barren woman in her
home as a happy mother of children.
Praise the Lord (Ps. 113:9).

The Best

Every night when the mother tucked her daughter in bed, the little girl said, "Mommy, your hair is beautiful. I love your hair. Mommy, your eyes are beautiful. I love your eyes. Mommy, your face is beautiful. I love your face. But Mommy your arms are ugly. I cannot love your arms."

One night when the mother was tucking in the little girl, she told her daughter that once when the daughter had been a tiny baby, there had been a fire in the house and the mother had reached through the flames to lift and carry her little girl to safety.

The little girl was quiet, then, she said, "Mommy, your hair is beautiful. I love it. Mommy, your eyes and your face are beautiful. I love them. But Mommy, your arms are the most beautiful of them all and I love them the best."

— Deanna Brown

People too often forget each other . . . but
everyone remembers Mother.

*Then his sister asked Pharaoh's
daughter, "Shall I go and get one of
the Hebrew women to nurse the baby
for you?" "Yes, go," she answered.
And the girl went and got the baby's
mother* (Exod. 2:8-9).

Mother Knows Best

A small boy sat with his mother in church, fidgeting, while listening to a sermon titled: "What is a Christian?" The preacher punctuated his message at several key intervals by asking the rhetorical question: "What is a Christian?" Each time he asked, he pounded his fist on the pulpit and pointed at someone in the audience for emphasis.

At one point, after the question had been asked a number of times, the little boy whispered to his mother, "Mama, do you know? Do you know what a Christian is?"

"Yes, my dear," the mother replied. "Now, please try to sit still and listen."

As the minister was moving to the wrap-up of the sermon, he thundered it once more, "What is a Christian?" and pounded especially hard on the pulpit and pointed in their direction.

At that, the boy jumped up and shouted, "Tell him, Mama, tell him!"

When a child pays attention to his mother,
she's probably whispering.

*The wolf will live with the lamb, the
leopard will lie down with the goat, the
calf and the lion and the yearling
together; and a little child will lead
them* (Isa. 11:6).

Perfection

Are you concerned about perfection? Think . . . IF things were right only 99.9 percent of the time, there would be: One hour of unsafe drinking water every month; two unsafe landings every day at Chicago's O'Hare Airport; 16,000 pieces of lost mail every hour; 20,000 incorrect drug prescriptions every year; 500 incorrect surgeries every week; 50 babies would be dropped on the floor at birth every day; 32,000 heartbeats per person would be missed per year; 22,000 checks would be deducted from the wrong checking account every hour! Now that's only IF things were right 99.9 percent of the time!

Personally, I'm thankful that things work as well as they do. There is only one person I know of that is 100 percent right 100 percent of the time. He's Divine! And He's God! And how all of us need a relationship with PERFECTION!

The most essential element in any
home is God.

*Before Me no god was formed, nor will
there be one after Me. I, even I, am the
Lord, and apart from Me there is no
savior* (Isa. 43:10-11).

The most important occupation on earth
for a woman is to be a real mother to her children.
It does not have much glory to it;
there is a lot of grit and grime.
But there is no greater place of ministry,
position, or power
than that of a mother.

Phil Whisenhunt

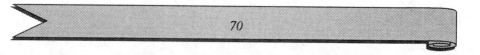

On Being Wrong

Thomas Huxley said, "Next to being right in this world, the best of all things is to be clearly and definitely wrong." Being wrong is a human art as old as any temple decoration. There are no facets of life which have not been touched by this oh-so-human capacity.

Consider just a few of the many possibilities:

Lord Byron in 1814 said, "Shakespeare's name, you may depend on it, stands absurdly too high and will go down!"

The *San Francisco Examiner*'s rejection letter to Rudyard Kipling said: "I'm sorry, Mr. Kipling, but you just don't know how to use the English language."

Then there was Mary Somerville, pioneer of radio educational broadcasts in 1948: "Television won't last. It's a flash in the pan!"

The woman who boasts that she never made a mistake likely has a husband who did.

If we claim to be without sin, we deceive ourselves and the truth is not in us. If we confess our sins, he is faithful and just and will forgive us our sins and purify us from all unrighteousness (1 John 1:8-9).

World's Fastest Failure

Until recently the world record for the fastest failure was held by Mrs. Helen Ireland of Auburn, California, who failed her driving test in the first second. How? By cleverly mistaking the accelerator for the clutch, stomping it to the floor, and shooting straight through the wall of the local driving test center.

This seemed unbeatable until an English auto mechanic from Lanarkshire named Thomas failed the test before the driver's license examiner had even gotten into the car. Arriving at the test center, Thomas tooted the horn to summon the examiner, who strode out to the vehicle, said it was illegal to sound your horn while stationary, announced that Thomas had failed, and strode back into the driving test center again!

Let's teach our children the art of careful planning!

It's true that to err is human . . . but it, too, can
be overdone.

*When the donkey saw the angel of the
Lord, she lay down under Balaam, and
he was angry and beat her with his
staff. Then the Lord opened the
donkey's mouth, and she said to
Balaam, "What have I done to you to
make you beat me these three times?"*
(Num. 22:27-28).

Ten Cannots

We are all familiar with the TEN COMMANDMENTS . . . let me share with you the following "TEN CANNOTS."

I. YOU CANNOT bring about prosperity by discouraging thrift.

II. YOU CANNOT help small people by tearing down big people.

III. YOU CANNOT strengthen the weak by weakening the strong.

IV. YOU CANNOT help the poor by destroying the rich.

V. YOU CANNOT keep out of financial trouble by spending more than your income.

VI. YOU CANNOT further brotherhood/sisterhood by inciting class hatred.

VII. YOU CANNOT establish financial security on borrowed money.

VIII. YOU CANNOT build character by taking away initiative and independence.

IX. YOU CANNOT help people by doing for them what they could do for themselves.

X. YOU CANNOT have a meaningful life without God.

The greatest thing in this world is not so much where we are, but in what direction we are moving. (O. W. Holmes)

Do not let this Book of the Law depart from your mouth; meditate on it day and night, so that you may be careful to do everything written in it. Then you will be prosperous and successful (Josh. 1:8).

If it was going to be easy to raise kids,
it never would have started
with something called labor.

Wonder Years

Are you aware that according to child psychologists the most difficult two years of life are the thirteenth and fourteenth years? It's a time when life is marked by rapid physical and emotional changes. Feelings of self-doubt and inferiority reach an all-time high during these years. An adolescent's worth as a human being hangs precariously on fickle peer group acceptance.

Relatively minor evidences of rejection or ridicule become significant to those who may already see themselves as fools and failures! Not being invited to an important event has a devastating impact, for example.

As mothers, grandmothers, and aunts we must remain in touch during these turbulent years. Let's not abandon our future resources to fickle peer pressure. We can start by sharing a good, encouraging word with the adolescents around us.

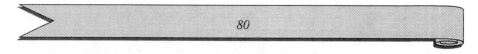

Adolescence is the period of growing up when children are positive they will never be as stupid as their parents.

Remember your Creator in the days of your youth, before the days of trouble come (Eccles. 12:1).

Discipline

A young mother, paying a visit to her doctor, was making no attempt to restrain her five-year-old son who was ransacking the adjoining examination room. Finally an extra loud crash of bottles did prompt her to say, "I hope you don't mind Johnny being in your examination room, Doctor."

"Not at all," replied the doctor, calmly, "he'll quiet down in a moment or two when he gets to the poison cabinet."

Discipline . . . we all like the end results but none of us really likes the process. If we, or anybody for that matter, are going to make it in life, there must be discipline, spiritual backbone, tenacity, perseverance, and good character, which are all traits that must be learned while people are still young. Kids are too young for self-discipline . . . therefore mothers as well as fathers are to be the disciplinarian force for kids.

The man who remembers what he learned at his mother's knee was probably bent over at the time.

Folly is bound up in the heart of a child, but the rod of discipline will drive it far from him (Prov. 22:15).

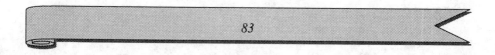

Mother's Prayer

Paul "Bear" Bryant, former football coach at the University of Alabama, now deceased, and I might add one of the best to ever coach the game, had one major regret over his coaching career. Neither his mother nor his father ever attended a football game he had played in or coached in.

But he liked to tell the story, often, about the prayer his mother prayed. It went like this: "Dear God, keep him from playing, but if he does, let him win."

One of the saddest situations I can remember is that when our own sons were competing athletically, many parents stayed away from an event that was so important to young people. It seems that Bear Bryant survived quite nicely . . . but will your own kids survive, if you neglect them in special times when they need your presence? God bless mothers who care enough to show up!

A diplomat is a mother with two kids on two
different Little League teams.

*She watches over the affairs of her
household and does not eat the bread
of idleness. Her children arise and call
her blessed* (Prov. 31:27-28).

*No job can compete
with the responsibility of
shaping and molding a new human being.*

James C. Dobson (1936–)

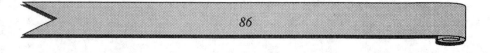

Silence Wins

Adele Faber, author of *How to Talk so Kids Will Listen,* tells how silence conquered the nightly battle over bedtime between mother and son, Jonathan, age eight. It had been ongoing for a long time, this nightly tussle. Here's how it played out.

One night Jonathan came downstairs as usual after being tucked into bed, "Mom, I can't sleep!" he said.

"Oh, you can't sleep. Hmmm," his mother replied. She stopped, looked at him with compassion and waited. A full minute passed without a word.

At last Jonathan spoke, "I think I'll put on my favorite pajamas," he said. "Then I'll sleep better." And off he went to bed and that was the last time there was a night-time go-to-bed battle. Let's learn when to listen and when to keep silent.

Every child has a right to be both
well-fed and well-led.

Be joyful in hope, patient in affliction,
faithful in prayer (Rom. 12:12).

Authority

A sixth grader comes home late from his suburban school and his mother is frantic. She asks, "What happened to you?"

The young man replied, "Well, I was made a traffic guard today, Mother, and all the kids have to wait for my signal after I stop a car before they can cross the street."

And his mother responded, "But you were supposed to be home two hours ago!"

Then he looks up to her and says, "Yes, but Mother, do you know how long I had to wait before a car came along that I could stop?"

It's about control. And don't we love to control and be in control of others? It's a very human trait we seem to be born with. But when we stop to think a moment or two . . . most of us have more problems with ourselves than adding the task of controlling others.

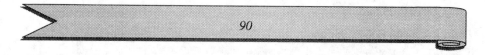

The happiest people are those who are too busy to notice whether they are in control or not.

Therefore, as God's chosen people, holy and dearly loved, clothe yourselves with compassion, kindness, humility, gentleness and patience (Col. 3:12).

Husbands

A very pregnant lady tells her husband he'd better get her to the hospital, quick! The first thing the nervous husband does is to run to the phone to call the hospital. He tells them he's bringing his wife in and they should notify everybody that she is about to have a baby!

The receptionist asks, "Is this her first baby?"

And the guy says, "Of course not. This is her husband!"

Ah, husbands, always cool in the face of an emergency, especially when the time comes for delivery of a baby! Being a husband and father is more than just being there. Being a mother is more than delivering a new baby. It's the sharing of responsibilities and taking an active part in parenting. It's doing the parenting together. Kids need mothers and fathers! When the Bible challenges to "train up a child" it implies that it takes both parents to do the job.

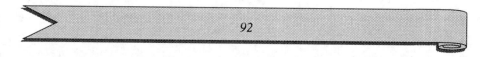

A real family is one who looks at their new child as an addition rather than a deduction.

So on that day Moses swore to me, "The land on which your feet have walked will be your inheritance and that of your children forever, because you have followed the Lord my God wholeheartedly" (Josh. 14:9).

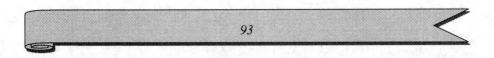

The school will teach children how to read,
but the environment of the home
must teach them what to read.
The school can teach them how to think,
but the home must teach them
what to believe.

Charles A. Wells

94

Mother's Golden Rules for Living

1) If you open it, close it. 2) If you turn it on, turn it off. 3) If you unlock it, lock it up. 4) If you break it, admit it. 5) If you can't fix it, call in someone who can. 6) If you borrow it, return it. 7) If you value it, take care of it. 8) If you make a mess, clean it up. 9) If you move it, put it back. 10) If it belongs to someone else and you want to use it, get permission. 11) If you don't know how to operate it, leave it alone. 12) If it's none of your business, don't ask questions. 13) If it isn't broke, don't fix it. 14) If it will brighten someone's day, say it. 15) If it will tarnish someone's reputation, keep it to yourself.

There you have them . . . 15 common-sense rules, really about all you'll ever need to get along in this life with others. Use them and pass them on.

Children are natural copycats — they act like their parents in spite of every effort to teach them good manners.

Therefore encourage one another and build each other up, just as in fact you are doing (1 Thess. 5:11).

Embarrassment

A young woman, very pregnant and overdue, had been rushed to the hospital, but not quite in time. She gave birth in the elevator of a North Carolina hospital while on her way to the labor room. This was quite an embarrassment to her because of all the good-natured kidding that went along with it, not to mention the publicity in the media. One of the nurses, in an effort to console her, said, "Don't feel bad. Why only about two years ago a lady delivered in the front yard of this hospital."

With that, the new mother burst out crying, "I know," she wailed, "that was me, too!"

To be embarrassed, according to *Random House Dictionary* is "to make uncomfortable, self-conscious; cause confusion and shame to; disconcert or abash." All of which is to say that it comes with being human. Embarrassed, lately? Do it with a smile and go on.

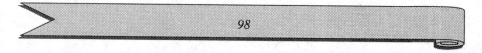

It is embarrassing to come to your senses only
to find out you haven't any.

*Blessed are the merciful, for they will
be shown mercy* (Matt. 5:7).

Roast Camel Recipe

One of the most complicated single dishes ever prepared by chefs is "roast-stuffed-camel"! About now, I've lost some of you, but let's go on. . . . This large, tasty delicacy is often served at large Bedouin marriage feasts.

The recipe reads: To prepare this delicacy, first take 100 gutted Mediterranean trout and stuff them with 200 hard-boiled eggs, then stuff the trout into 50 cooked chickens. The chickens are then placed into the body cavity of a sheep and the sheep into the carcass of a camel. Roast over a charcoal fire until done. It serves about 300 guests.

I kid you not, this recipe is taken from *The Book of Strange Facts and Useless Information*. So, Mom, when the next marriage feast is about to take place in your family . . . you now have a new recipe that will both titillate and cause a sensation among the invited guests!

Psychiatrists tell us that girls tend to marry men who are like their fathers. . . . So now we know why it is that mothers cry at weddings.

> *"Tell those who have been invited that*
> *I have prepared my dinner: My oxen*
> *and fattened cattle have been*
> *butchered, and everything is ready.*
> *Come to the wedding banquet"*
> (Matt. 22:4).

Countless times each day a mother does
what no one else can do quite as well.
She wipes away a tear, whispers a word of hope,
eases a child's fears. She teaches, ministers, loves,
and nurtures the next generation of citizens.
And she challenges and cajoles her kids to do their
best and be the best. But no editorials
praise these accomplishments — where is the
coverage our mothers rightfully deserve?

James C. Dobson (1936–)
and Gary L. Bauer (1946–)

Handicapped

Jeff Resler played guard for the University of Oklahoma football team in the offensive line. He also bench presses over 400 pounds. He is 6'-2" tall and weighs 260 pounds. You're thinking, *Well, what's so special about that?* Jeff is a young man without the use of a left hand since birth. The hand was malformed and had to be amputated to avoid infection.

His parents encouraged him to participate in any activity he wanted to. The only accommodation was that his mother replaced the buttons on his shirts with snaps. There was no pity, no poor-little-you kind of words. They were positive, they re-affirmed, they encouraged, they challenged, and they loved Jeff so that he was able to achieve in life.

Jeff says, "My parents never told me I COULDN'T do anything!" And with a smile, he adds, "I can usually do what I set my mind to."

Unless you try to do something beyond what
you have already mastered, you will never
grow. (Ronald E. Osborn)

I press on toward the goal to win the
prize for which God has called me
heavenward in Christ Jesus
(Phil. 3:14).

Women in Uniform

Catherine G. Lutes of Tallmadge, Ohio, tells this: During basic training for the army nurse corps, we were required to spend one week in the field roughing it. It rained the entire week. We arose daily in our swampy tent, took a cold water beauty bath from our helmets, donned our pistol belts and ponchos, and trudged through the mud to set up field hospitals. Obviously, our personal appearance frequently left much to be desired.

The final blow to our feminine pride occurred while we waited in the mess line in the mud and rain. A young private came by with a camera and asked to take our picture. "It will prove to my girl," he said, "that she has NO reason to be jealous."

Maybe this being a mother isn't all that bad! If we stop and think . . . it could be worse, so why not enjoy the present and be thankful for the ladies in uniform, too.

Service is nothing else than love
in work clothes.

Finally, be strong in the Lord and in
His mighty power. Put on the full
armor of God so that you can take
your stand (Eph. 6:10).

Airline Attendants

Here are some recently recorded announcements of various airline flight attendants:

In GERMANY: "Good evening. Welcome to the world's superior airline. Please march to your seats, sit without squirming, ring for the hostess only when absolutely necessary."

In ISRAEL: "We shall be flying at an altitude . . . you wouldn't believe it! Under your seat is a life jacket. You should wear it only in good health."

In MADRID: "Have a most pleasant flight and please pray for clear skies because the planes in Spain fall mainly in the rains."

Then . . . there was the mother who told her flight attendant, "Please tell the pilot not to fly faster than sound. My friend and I want to be able to talk."

It's a marvelous, technologically advanced age we live in . . . but it still takes people to make the world go round.

Dear God, I hope You'll also take care of yourself. If anything should happen to You, we'd be in an awful fix. (A child's prayer)

Pray also for me, that whenever I open my mouth, words may be given me (Eph. 6:19).

If you enjoyed this book, we also have available:

Mini-Moments for Fathers
Mini-Moments for Graduates

and coming soon:

Mini-Moments for Christmas

Available at bookstores nationwide or write:
New Leaf Press, P.O. Box 726, Green Forest, AR 72638